SUFFRAGETTES
AND THE
FIGHT
FOR THE
VOTE

Sarah Ridley

W
FRANKLIN WATTS
LONDON · SYDNEY

Franklin Watts
First published in Great Britain in 2017 by
The Watts Publishing Group

Credits
Editor: Sarah Peutrill
Designer: Jeni Child

ISBN 978 1 4451 5261 5

Printed in China

Franklin Watts
An imprint of
Hachette Children's Group
Part of The Watts Publishing Group
Carmelite House
50 Victoria Embankment
London EC4Y 0DZ

An Hachette UK Company
www.hachette.co.uk

www.franklinwatts.co.uk

Picture credits:
All images from the LSE Digital Library with the exception
of those listed below.

Antique Print Gallery/Alamy: 13bl.British Library
Board, London: 25t. British Museum, London: 29t. Lt.
Ernest Brooks/ Imperial War Museum: 42l. © Crown
Copyright. The National Archives: 35l. Mary Evans PL:
5, 44. GL Archive/Alamy: 6tl, 11b. Houses of Parliament
Archives,HC/SA/SJ/3/1 :18. ILN/Mary Evans PL:
7tlb, 43b. Imperial War Museum, London: 41b, 42r, 43t.
Lavenham Exhibition and Museum Trust: 40. Library of
Congress: 6bra. Museum of London PL: front cover, 14,16b,
20, 21tl, 23, 24, 27b, 28t, 29c, 29b, 31b, 33b, 34, 35r, 38,
39c. National Portrait Gallery, London: 39b. The March
of the Women Collection/ Mary Evans PL: 4, 19c. WHA/
Alamy: 12. CC Wikimedia Commons: 6tr, 7tr, 36.

Every attempt has been made to clear copyright. Should
there be any inadvertent omission please apply to the
publisher for rectification.

CONTENTS

A man's world	4
The key people	6
The Petition	8
Suffrage societies	10
The Women's Social and Political Union	14
The Women's Freedom League	18
Deeds not words	20
Hunger strikes	22
Newspapers	24
Fund raising and propaganda	26
Processions, marches and rallies	30
Banners	32
No vote, no census	34
Derby Day, 1913	36
Scaling up the action	38
The First World War	40
The Vote!	44
Glossary	46
Timeline/Index	48

A MAN'S WORLD

ORIGIN AND DEVELOPMENT OF A SUFFRAGETTE.

At 15 a little Pet.

At 20 a little Coquette

At 40 not married yet!

At 50 A Suffragette.

VOTES FOR WOMEN

Today every British citizen, male or female, who is over the age of 18 has the right to vote in elections. Most people take this right for granted. However, if you had been born in the 19th or early 20th centuries you would have witnessed the long, hard struggle of women trying to persuade men to give them the vote. Campaigners were often depicted in a negative way, as here on this early 20th century postcard, which records the transformation from teenager to spinster (unmarried) suffragette!

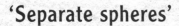

'Separate spheres'

During the 19th century, it was generally accepted that men and women should occupy 'separate spheres', living very different lives. Women were seen to have weaker bodies but a stronger sense of right and wrong, making them ideal for running the home and bringing up children in the 'private sphere'. Men, on the other hand, lived in the 'public sphere' of work and politics. All women were under the control of their male relatives, their father, brother or husband.

Campaigning women

Some women challenged their role in society in different ways. They campaigned alongside men to extend suffrage, the power to vote, to a wider group of people. At that time, it was mostly wealthy landowners who voted to elect Members of Parliament (MPs). Campaigners hoped that if a wider group of people in society had the right to vote, they could use that power to influence MPs to change the law and guide the government to make society fairer for all, rather than for the few. However, political reform was strongly resisted by many in power.

In 1819 women joined a peaceful demonstration in St Peter's Field, Manchester asking for reform. It became known as the 'Peterloo Massacre' after soldiers killed 11 and injured about 400 protesters.

The Great Reform Act, 1832

Finally, a bill to reform the electoral system was introduced into Parliament and eventually became law in the form of the Great Reform Act of 1832. The number of people eligible to vote rose from about 366,000 to 650,000. The new voters were men who fulfilled a new property qualification, as well as some tenant farmers and shopkeepers. In addition, citizens of cities such as Manchester and Birmingham gained MPs to represent them for the first time. However, the wording of the Reform Act specifically excluded women from the vote.

After the Great Reform Act, women did not give up on the idea of gaining the vote but, for some, the need for change in other areas of women's lives was just as important. They wanted better education, job opportunities and equal treatment in law courts. Many women came to the conclusion that if women had the right to vote, they could use this political power to bring changes across society.

Bills, acts and laws

Citizens of a country have to follow the laws of that country, such as not committing crimes or making sure that children receive an education. In the United Kingdom:

- Each law begins as a bill.
- A bill is a detailed draft of a new law or a proposal to change an existing law, introduced by a government department or an individual MP.
- Members of the House of Commons and the House of Lords discuss the bill, make changes and eventually, if agreement is reached, the bill becomes an act. And so a new law, or an amendment to a law, comes into being.

THE KEY PEOPLE

Elizabeth Garrett Anderson

Elizabeth was an active supporter of the campaign for votes for women, starting with the 1866 Petition. Overcoming many hurdles, she became the first English woman to qualify as a doctor. She married and had three children.

1836–1917

Herbert Henry Asquith

Herbert was elected as a Liberal MP in 1886 and, right from the beginning, he expressed his opposition to votes for women. He was prime minister from 1908–1916, often using his position to block votes for women.

1852–1928

Viscountess Nancy Astor

Born in the USA, Nancy married the British politician Waldorf Astor. After he inherited the title of Viscount and stopped being an MP, she was elected to his seat in 1919 and became the first woman MP to sit in the House of Commons.

1879–1964

Lydia Becker

Lydia was involved in the Manchester National Society for Women's Suffrage from when it was set up in 1867, and became its leader. She edited the *Women's Suffrage Journal,* and was a respected astronomer and botanist.

1827–1890

Teresa Billington-Greig

A friend of Emmeline Pankhurst, Teresa gave up teaching to devote herself to the WSPU, the Independent Labour Party and later the WFL. She was known for whirling a whip over her head to stop people from evicting her from meetings!

1877–1964

Emily Davies

Emily was a friend of Elizabeth Garrett Anderson and encouraged her to study medicine. She campaigned for women and girls to have access to a good education and also supported the women's suffrage movement.

1830–1921

Emily Wilding Davison

A university graduate, Emily was a teacher before she decided to devote herself to women's suffrage. A member of the WSPU, she carried out various acts to draw attention to the cause, including stepping in front of King George V's horse.

1872–1913

Charlotte Despard

Charlotte was born in Edinburgh and was a well-known social reformer, working to improve the lives of the poor. Originally a member of the WSPU, she helped found the Women's Freedom League and became its first president.

1844–1939

Flora Drummond

Born in Manchester, Flora grew up in the Scottish Highlands. She became one of the WSPU's main organisers and took part in many WSPU actions, gaining the nickname 'the General' for riding her horse at the front of processions.

1879–1949

Millicent Garrett Fawcett

Millicent, younger sister of Elizabeth Garrett Anderson, juggled marriage to an MP, Henry Fawcett, motherhood and work for the London Society for Women's Suffrage, eventually leading the NUWSS when it was formed in 1897.

1847–1929

Laurence Housman

Laurence was a founding member of the Men's League for Women's Suffrage. He became a skilled writer and illustrator after he left the Royal College of Art and helped to found the Suffrage Atelier, a group of artists and designers.

1865–1959

Annie Kenney

Born in Lancashire, Annie left her job in a cotton mill to devote herself to the WSPU. She was the only working-class woman to be part of the leadership of the organisation, and felt great loyalty to Emmeline and Christabel Pankhurst.

1879–1953

David Lloyd George

Brought up in Wales, David was elected as a Liberal MP in 1890. During the First World War he was Minister of Munitions. Although he supported votes for women, he didn't always speak out but he was the prime minister who saw the Representation of the People Act become law in 1918.

1863–1945

Lady Constance Lytton

Constance joined the WSPU after she met Emmeline Pethick-Lawrence and Annie Kenney. She took part in deputations to the Houses of Parliament and other actions, which resulted in several prison sentences.

1869–1923

J S Mill

John Stuart Mill was a philosopher, social reformer and MP whose ideas influenced many people during his life and are still discussed today. He supported the campaign for votes for women, presenting the 1866 Petition to Parliament.

1806–1873

Christabel Pankhurst

The eldest daughter of Emmeline Pankhurst, Christabel had a degree in law but, like all female law graduates, was not allowed to work as a lawyer. She devoted herself to the WSPU, and was a brilliant public speaker and leader.

1880–1958

Emmeline Pankhurst

Born in Manchester, Emmeline married Dr Richard Pankhurst. She set up the WSPU in 1903 and was a great inspiration to women through her speeches and her willingness to make sacrifices for the cause. She went to prison numerous times and was force fed.

1858–1928

Sylvia Pankhurst

Sylvia was the daughter of Emmeline and sister to Christabel Pankhurst. She came to question her mother and sister's leadership of the WSPU and helped set up the East London Federation of Suffragettes in 1913.

1882–1960

Pethick-Lawrences

Emmeline (left) and Frederick Pethick-Lawrence offered financial and leadership skills to the WSPU until 1912, and jointly edited *Votes for Women*. Frederick (1871–1961) used his legal skills on many occasions to advise members of the WSPU.

1867 1954

Princess Sophia Duleep Singh

A daughter of an Indian Maharajah and a goddaughter of Queen Victoria, Princess Sophia joined the WSPU. She spoke at meetings, sold the *Suffragette* newspaper, joined deputations and processions and took part in direct actions.

(c.1876–1948)

The women's suffrage movement had the support of thousands of women and men across the country whose names are largely forgotten. These biographies give brief details about some of the people mentioned in this book.

THE PETITION

In 1866 a small group of women organised a petition asking MPs to extend the right to vote equally to men and unmarried women who owned property. It marked the real beginning of the campaign for women's suffrage. This painting by Bertha Newcombe, painted in 1910, captures the moment when Elizabeth Garrett and Emily Davies were about to give the Petition to John Stuart Mill, a supportive MP. The women had hidden the Petition under an apple-seller's stall in Westminster Hall to avoid attracting attention.

Organising the Petition

Elizabeth Garrett (married name: Anderson) and Emily Davies belonged to a group of women who met at Langham Place, London, in the 1850s and 1860s. After a discussion about suffrage in 1865, some of them formed the Women's Suffrage Committee in order to organise a petition asking for votes for women. The committee met at Elizabeth Garrett's home and her sister, Millicent, helped gather signatures.

The Petition had been written with great care. It asked for the vote to be extended to 'all householders, without distinction of sex, who possess such property and rental qualifications as your honourable House may determine.' This would include female homeowners but exclude married women, which it was hoped would help make it appeal to more MPs.

The Petition was in the form of a long scroll but Emily Davies also had it made into a pamphlet, shown here, that was posted to all MPs and to newspapers.

Collecting signatures

MP John Stuart Mill agreed to present the Petition to Parliament if the women could get at least a hundred signatures. In just two weeks they collected 1,499 signatures using their family and friendship networks. Alongside the friends, relatives and neighbours of the committee members are the signatures of women in their communities: teachers, shopkeepers, dressmakers, and the wives of butchers, greengrocers and blacksmiths. In June 1866 John Stuart Mill presented the Petition to Parliament, but no debate took place. Public petitions are still a way for citizens to ask MPs in the House of Commons to debate an issue which concerns them.

John Stuart Mill appeared on this postcard, produced by the Women's Freedom League (see pages 18–19).

Second Reform Bill, 1867

A year later, in May 1867, the Petition led to John Stuart Mill giving a speech in the House of Commons, where the issue of Parliamentary reform was once again being considered in the form of the Second Reform Bill. He tried to persuade MPs to amend (make a change) to the Second Reform Bill, asking for the word 'person' to replace the word 'man', which would have led to the vote being extended to some women. Although the amendment was defeated by 196 votes to 73, this showed a good level of support across political parties. When it was passed, the Second Reform Act gave about a million more men, some of them working class, the right to vote. Between 1866 and 1918, more than 16,000 petitions asking for women to be given the vote were presented to Parliament.

SUFFRAGE SOCIETIES

A year after the 1866 Petition, the first suffrage societies were set up in London, Manchester and Edinburgh. Millicent Garrett Fawcett was a founding member of the London National Society for Women's Suffrage. In 1867 Millicent married the blind MP, Henry Fawcett, a supporter of women's suffrage, photographed here with Millicent in about 1880. Millicent remained involved in the campaign for votes for women all her life, eventually becoming the leader of the National Union of Women's Suffrage Societies (see page 13).

Methods of campaigning

Soon there were suffrage societies across the country, in towns as well as cities. Members of the societies met in private houses and public halls and continued to discuss how to achieve the goal of votes for women. Mostly this involved presenting more signed petitions to MPs and producing pamphlets or posters to explain to others why women should be given the vote. Suffragists always campaigned peacefully, hoping to gradually win the support of politicians and members of the public.

Millicent Garrett Fawcett and other suffragists travelled around the country, speaking at public meetings to draw attention to the cause. Many of the women were unused to public speaking, but gradually their experience grew. Millicent Garrett Fawcett's technique was to list all the reasons that people gave as to why women were not to be allowed the vote – and then to demolish them one by one.

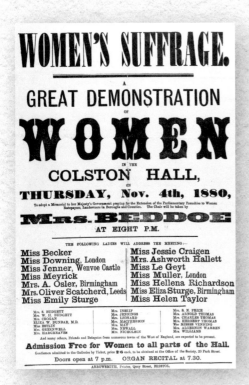

 This poster advertises a 'great demonstration' organised by Bristol and West of England Society for Women's Suffrage, formed in 1868. It was attended by more than 3,000 people.

Busy women

Women involved in the suffrage campaign were often campaigning for change in other areas of society, too. Emily Davies, who had jointly presented the 1866 Petition, devoted much of her time to improving education for girls and women, working to persuade people that girls and women needed a good education, including the right to attend university. Meanwhile, other women spent most of their available time trying to gain women access to a medical career (Elizabeth Garrett), overturn the Contagious Diseases Act (Josephine Butler) or contribute to other important campaigns.

Elizabeth Garrett Anderson campaigned for women's suffrage and for women to access a medical career while also studying medicine.

Manchester Society

Led by Lydia Becker, the Manchester Society, officially known as the National Society for Women's Suffrage, quickly became the most influential suffrage society in the mid 19th century. Members wanted to gain the vote for all women, married or single, rather than limiting themselves to the more modest aims of the 1866 Petition. They also worked on a new plan: to use the existing laws to prove that some women already had the right to have their name on the electoral register. Despite their efforts, only one woman voted before the law was changed.

Jacob Bright

In Parliament, the MP for Manchester, Jacob Bright, had taken over from John Stuart Mill as a campaigner for votes for women. He presented a suffrage bill to Parliament in 1870, asking for the vote to be given to women who owned property. It got through the first stage but was then blocked by Prime Minister Gladstone. He wasn't the only one to disapprove of the bill. The reigning monarch, Queen Victoria, was against women's suffrage and wrote in 1870: "Let women be what God intended, a helpmate for man, but with totally different duties and vocations."

▽ In 1871, *Punch* magazine printed this cartoon showing Lydia Becker (see page 11), wrapped in the Suffrage Bill, being thrown out of Parliament. Newspapers often printed cartoons mocking the suffragists.

Political parties

In 1871 another suffrage bill was presented to Parliament and, yet again, it failed to gain the support of enough MPs, as occurred again in debates leading up to the Third Reform Act of 1884. The 1884 Reform Act meant that two-thirds of men over the age of 21 now had the vote. The suffragists had assumed that the Liberal Party would help them get the vote, as many Liberals supported women's suffrage. However, it became clear that their leader, William Gladstone, did not support women's suffrage, partly because he believed that the new women voters would support the opposition, the Conservative Party. As for the Conservatives, the party leaders repeatedly stated their support for votes for women, but many Conservative MPs were against the idea and the leadership did nothing to introduce changes to the law when they had the power to do so.

Meanwhile, during the 1890s, the Manchester Society (see page 11) recruited working-class women by giving speeches at factory gates. It also built links with the newly formed Independent Labour Party (ILP). Unlike other political parties, the ILP officially accepted women on an equal basis to men.

Anti-suffragists

In 1889 more trouble for the women's suffrage movement came in the form of organised opposition from women. Mary Ward, a published author, drafted an appeal 'Against the Extension of Parliamentary Franchise to Women' which was signed by many notable women of the day. Their argument was that women should not participate in politics or it would break down the difference between men and women. Unfortunately many across society, male and female, quietly agreed with this argument.

A national society

Suffrage societies were established all across the UK. Some joined together and split apart again, but there was no national society until 1897, when 17 of the largest suffrage societies came together to be part of the National Union of Women's Suffrage Societies. The cover of a NUWSS leaflet produced in 1913 (right) illustrates what this meant, with the suffrage societies tracing their link back to the first societies formed in 1867, the date in the acorn. From this acorn, all the other societies have grown, represented by the NUWSS tree with the names of the societies written on branches. Millicent Garrett Fawcett was their leader and officially became the union's president in 1907.

> The cover of a NUWSS leaflet produced in 1913. The numbers in the leaves refer to the federations – groups of societies.

⚠ In 1869, Britain's first women's college opened with five students in Hitchin, Hertfordshire. In 1873 it moved to Girton, Cambridge, pictured here in 1907.

Progress check

Slowly, women's position in society was improving. For example, by the end of the 19th century women were permitted by law to keep their own property and money after marriage. Some girls' schools had been established, the first women had attended university and a few (including Elizabeth Garrett Anderson – see pages 6, 8–9 and 11) even managed to become doctors. At a local level, women were allowed to sit on School Boards, and vote in local elections. But after 40 years of campaigning, women had made almost no progress in the campaign to gain the vote for women in national elections.

THE WOMEN'S SOCIAL AND POLITICAL UNION

As time passed and the efforts of the suffrage societies had still not resulted in votes for women, some women started to think that the time had come to use different tactics. One of them, Emmeline Pankhurst, set up a new organisation called the Women's Social and Political Union (WSPU) in 1903. Emmeline, pictured here on a fund-raising brooch, was the widow of Dr Richard Pankhurst, a lawyer and supporter of women's suffrage. Their daughters, Christabel and Sylvia, were leading members of the WSPU, which at first met in their family home in Manchester.

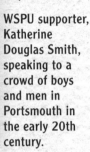

WSPU supporter, Katherine Douglas Smith, speaking to a crowd of boys and men in Portsmouth in the early 20th century.

'Deeds not Words'

Adopting the motto 'Deeds not Words', the WSPU demanded that MPs change the law rather than repeat promises about how women would eventually get the vote. At first the WSPU campaigned in the same way as the NUWSS, holding meetings, giving speeches in public, putting up posters and distributing pamphlets.

Unlike the NUWSS, which allowed men to be members, the WSPU was a women-only organisation, and they were small in number, with only about 30 members by mid 1905. At this point, most of the members were working-class women who belonged to the Independent Labour Party (see page 12), but the Pankhurst family kept tight control of decision-making. Members gave speeches at factory gates and in public places, trying to gain support for the campaign for votes for women from men and women alike.

First militant act

In 1905, frustrated by the government's lack of response to the suffrage movement, the WSPU organised its first militant, or forceful, act, interpreting their motto of 'Deeds not Words' in a different way. Christabel Pankhurst and Annie Kenney, a former mill worker and member of the WSPU, went to the Free Trade Hall in Manchester where the Liberal Party was holding a meeting. They repeatedly interrupted the speaker to ask, "Will the Liberal government give women the vote?" In the end, they were forced to leave the hall, were arrested and were eventually sent to prison. Everything was reported in the newspapers – the WSPU had found a way to gain free publicity.

Annie Kenney (left) and Christabel Pankhurst. Christabel was highly charismatic and attracted passionate support from others.

From Manchester to London

In 1906 the WSPU headquarters moved from Manchester to London. The Pankhursts wanted to focus their attention on politicians and it was much easier to do this when MPs were on their way to, or on their way back from, the Houses of Parliament. They set up their new office in the London home of Emmeline and Frederick Pethick-Lawrence, who also gave financial support to the WSPU.

The women planned actions and meetings, demonstrations and processions. Some women chalked messages on London pavements, advertising meetings nearby, or printed tickets for organised events in halls or outdoors. They wrote and printed pamphlets, books and the weekly newspaper, *Votes for Women* (see pages 24–25), and raised money for the cause in various ways.

A meeting of WSPU leaders in about 1906 in their new offices in the Pethick-Lawrences' home. From left to right: Flora Drummond, Christabel Pankhurst, Annie Kenney, Nellie Martel, Emmeline Pankhurst, Charlotte Despard, unidentified (profile).

Campaigning

WSPU members stopped politicians on the street to try to speak to them about votes for women, they shouted comments at them in public places and interrupted meetings in London and across the country. Groups of women repeatedly went to the Houses of Parliament to ask MPs to debate the issue of votes for women. In 1906 they gained the name 'suffragette' from a negative *Daily Mail* article about a group of WSPU women who tried to speak to the prime minister. Later, the WSPU adopted the word, describing themselves as suffragettes.

Suffragettes were photographed pestering Prime Minister Asquith as he walked along Downing Street in 1908.

Why go to prison?

It was the suffragettes' intention to constantly break the law in small ways, and be sent to prison by refusing to pay the fines that most people were prepared to pay in order to avoid imprisonment. The aim was to cause inconvenience to the government, which didn't want prisons clogged up with women serving short prison sentences. In addition, the government wanted to avoid attracting the bad publicity gained by newspaper articles reporting the arrest and imprisonment of suffragette prisoners.

After serving a prison sentence, women were usually released first thing in the morning. Crowds of supporters greeted them and processed through the streets to breakfast parties, creating another opportunity for free publicity as newspapers reported the events.

Police arrested Emmeline and Christabel Pankhurst and Flora Drummond at the WSPU office in October 1908 to prevent them from taking part in a 'rush' on Parliament, when 60,000 women tried to enter Parliament.

In 1908 Edith New and Mary Leigh were jailed for smashing windows. This photo captures their release, greeted by a crowd of supporters.

Suffragette and suffragist

In the early years of the 20th century, some women belonged to both types of organisation – a suffrage society, such as the NUWSS, as well as the WSPU, or even moved between them. After all, all the organisations were working for the same end result: votes for women on the same terms as they were given to men. For instance, Elizabeth Garrett Anderson, who had jointly presented the 1866 Petition (see pages 8–9) and had been a law-abiding suffragist most of her life, decided to join the WSPU in 1908, becoming a suffragette at the age of 72. However, she withdrew her support in 1911 in protest at the WSPU's arson campaign (see pages 38–39). Whether women supported the suffragists or the suffragettes, WSPU tactics resulted in a rise in membership for all suffrage organisations across the country.

However, as time went on and some members of the WSPU committed ever more violent acts, Millicent Garrett Fawcett and the NUWSS worried that WSPU tactics might be working against the cause, losing the support of MPs who had previously pledged their support. And it wasn't just members of other suffrage organisations that had begun to question the leadership of the WSPU. Some members of the WSPU had split from the organisation in 1907 and formed the Women's Freedom League (WFL) (see next page).

THE WOMEN'S FREEDOM LEAGUE

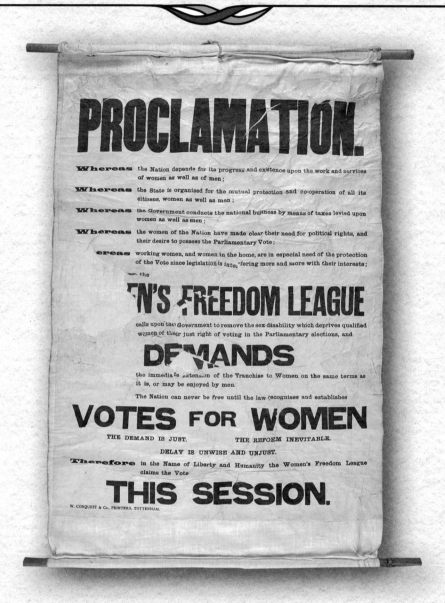

PROCLAMATION.

Whereas the Nation depends for its progress and existence upon the work and services of women as well as of men;

Whereas the State is organised for the mutual protection and co-operation of all its citizens, women as well as men;

Whereas the Government conducts the national business by means of taxes levied upon women as well as men;

Whereas the women of the Nation have made clear their need for political rights, and their desire to possess the Parliamentary Vote;

Whereas working women, and women in the home, are in especial need of the protection of the Vote since legislation is interfering more and more with their interests;

the WOMEN'S FREEDOM LEAGUE

calls upon the Government to remove the sex-disability which deprives qualified women of their just right of voting in the Parliamentary elections, and

DEMANDS

the immediate extension of the Franchise to Women on the same terms as it is, or may be enjoyed by men.

The Nation can never be free until the law recognises and establishes

VOTES FOR WOMEN

THE DEMAND IS JUST.   THE REFORM INEVITABLE.

DELAY IS UNWISE AND UNJUST.

Therefore in the Name of Liberty and Humanity the Women's Freedom League claims the Vote

THIS SESSION.

W. CONQUEST & Co., PRINTERS, TOTTENHAM.

On 28 October 1908 members of the Women's Freedom League smuggled this banner, created by sticking a poster to a piece of cloth, into the Ladies Gallery of the House of Commons. They poked it through a metal grill and unfurled it so that MPs down below could read their demands. Two women chained themselves to the grille, which had to be removed with them still attached to it before officials could cut them free!

A WFL badge showing their official colours. It was sold to raise funds and worn as a form of propaganda.

Who belonged to the Women's Freedom League?

Many of the women who belonged to the Women's Freedom League (WFL) had previously belonged to the WSPU. They included Teresa Billington-Greig and Charlotte Despard (see page 6), who set up the WFL in 1907 because they did not like the way the WSPU was dominated by the Pankhursts and the Pethick-Lawrences. By contrast, the WFL was a democratic organisation, committed to campaigning for votes for women without the use of violence, although they were still prepared to break the law to attract attention to the cause.

WFL actions

In response to Prime Minister Asquith's refusal to meet with members to discuss women's suffrage the WFL set up 'The Great Watch'. This meant the continuous presence of women outside the House of Commons from July to November, 1909, and a similar action outside 10 Downing Street, the official home of the prime minister. Members of the WFL took part in the huge NUWSS march in June 1908 and the Coronation Procession in 1911 (see pages 30–31). They also destroyed ballot papers during the Bermondsey by-election in 1909, produced leaflets, posters and pamphlets to try to change people's minds about women's suffrage and published their own newspaper called the *Vote*.

Muriel Matters of the WFL even took to the air in 1909, dropping leaflets down to Londoners from an airship emblazoned with the words WOMEN'S FREEDOM LEAGUE and VOTES FOR WOMEN! Muriel was one of the women who chained herself to the grille in the Ladies Gallery (see left) and she also went 'vanning', touring the countryside in a WFL caravan to

This Women's Freedom League postcard shows Muriel Matters (left) standing on the step of a WFL caravan in 1908. Supporters of the NUWSS also used caravan tours to gather support for the cause.

spread the word about women's suffrage at outdoor meetings. Although WFL speakers often found themselves drowned out by the heckles (whistles and shouts) of men and boys, several new branches of the WFL sprang up in the wake of these tours.

Taxes and the Census

The WFL set up a sister organisation called the Women's Tax Resistance League. Members of the league refused to pay a variety of taxes until women were granted the vote. This led to bailiffs seizing the goods of women in place of payment of the taxes, and imprisonment for some. The idea of using the 1911 census as a form of protest also came from the WFL originally (see pages 34–35 for more on this).

A badge produced by the Women's Tax Resistance League to spread the word about their campaign.

DEEDS NOT WORDS

Direct action, such as chaining themselves to monuments or railings in busy places, was one way that members of the WFL and the WSPU drew attention to their cause. To do this, a woman often wore a thick belt and used padlocks and chains, including this one (right), to attach the belt and herself to the railings. Chained in place, the woman started to deliver a speech, or shout at the prime minister or an MP, until the police managed to cut the chains.

10 Downing Street

In 1908 Edith New and Olivia Smith chained themselves to the railings outside 10 Downing Street. While they shouted, "Votes for Women," another suffragette, Flora Drummond, tried to enter the building and disrupt a cabinet meeting. After the police had cut the chains, all the women were arrested and charged with disorderly behaviour. They were ordered to pay a fine as punishment for breaking the law, but they chose a prison sentence instead.

Three women, carrying padlock and chains inside the rolls, prepare to chain themselves to railings in 1909.

Window-smashing

10 Downing Street was the focus of another 'deed', also carried out in 1908. This time it involved smashing the windows of the prime minster's house. Later, in court, the window-smashers, Mary Leigh and Edith New, said they had carried out this criminal damage as a response to the police treating protestors harshly at a WSPU demonstration nearby. Window-smashing was taken up as a form of action by suffragettes all across the country, causing a lot of damage.

Holloway brooch

'Deeds' often ended in a prison sentence and so, in 1909, the WSPU started presenting ex-prisoners with a Holloway brooch, to honour their sacrifice of personal liberty. Hundreds of suffragettes were imprisoned in the women-only Holloway prison between 1906 and 1914, and of course in other prisons across the country.

The Holloway brooch was designed by Sylvia Pankhurst. It consists of the portcullis symbol of the House of Commons and chains, with the convict arrow on the front.

Black Friday

Peaceful protests when no one broke the law could also end badly for the women involved. During most of 1910, the WSPU had stopped militant action while politicians considered the Conciliation Bill, which offered the hope of the vote to a narrow group of women. When Prime Minister Asquith stopped the bill from becoming an act, the WSPU were furious. As a response, they sent a deputation of 300 women to the Houses of Parliament. Police clashed with the women and treated them very roughly during a six-hour struggle, leading to the day being called Black Friday. Over a hundred women were arrested.

The arrest of a suffragette on Black Friday, 18 November 1910. Women suffered black eyes, broken bones, bruising and acts of sexual violence inflicted by policemen and some men from the crowd who joined in.

HUNGER STRIKES

In the summer of 1909 the first suffragette prisoners went on hunger strike. This meant they refused all food, which forced the prison authorities to release them after a few days. In August that year, the WSPU presented the first hunger strike medals to women on their release from prison. The medals were inscribed with the words 'For Valour' and 'Hunger Strike'. This medal (above) was presented to Elsie Duval in 1912. She was sent to Holloway prison for a month for breaking a post-office window in March 1912.

Hunger strikers

Acting alone in July 1909, Marion Wallace Dunlop was the first suffragette to go on hunger strike. Suffragettes were not ordered to go on hunger strike by the leadership but took that decision themselves. The women wanted to be recognised as political prisoners rather than criminals, which would have given them the right to better treatment in the first division in prison. At this time prisons were divided into three divisions according to the crime, with the first division prisoners given better living conditions, uniforms and treatment than those in the lower divisions.

Force feeding

As an increasing number of women prisoners went on hunger strike, the government became concerned that one of them might die and become a martyr to the cause. So in September 1909, they directed prison staff to force feed hunger strikers. As shown on the poster, the prisoner was held down so that a doctor could force a rubber feeding tube down her throat or up her nose. Using a funnel, liquid food was poured down the tube and into the stomach. Some women experienced the horror of force feeding hundreds of times.

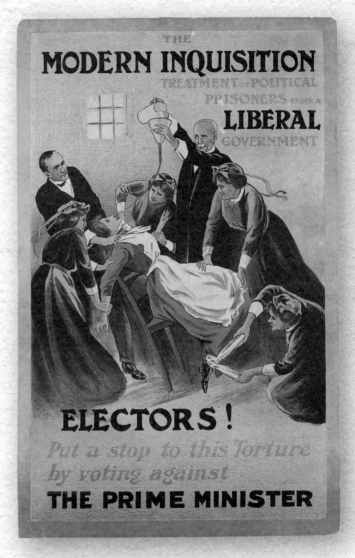

This WSPU poster showing force feeding was issued in 1910 in the run up to a general election. It urges voters to vote against the Liberal government.

Painful and dangerous

Many women had their health ruined by force feeding. Sometimes the liquid food ended up in their lungs rather than their stomach, causing infections. Force feeding caused women to choke, bruised and scratched their throats and could permanently damage their health.

Middle-class suffragettes were treated more gently than working-class women who had committed the same crimes. Lady Constance Lytton proved this by giving a false name, Jane Warton, when she was arrested in 1910. As Jane, she served 14 days in the third division, rather than the second, and was force fed eight times without any medical checks (she had a heart condition). When she was arrested under her own name, she was given medical checks and was released after a few days 'on health grounds'.

In recognition of the additional sacrifice made by hunger strikers who were force fed, the WSPU added bars to women's hunger strike medals. Elsie Duval's medal (left) has two bars across it, representing the two prison sentences during which she was force fed on a number of occasions.

23

NEWSPAPERS

To give themselves a voice, suffrage organisations set up their own newspapers and journals, of which *Votes for Women*, the official newspaper of the WSPU, was the most famous and effective. It started in 1907 and was published by the husband and wife team, Frederick and Emmeline Pethick-Lawrence. This poster, designed by Hilda Dallas in 1909, advertised the newspaper. It uses the WSPU colours of green, white and purple and depicts a suffragette newspaper seller wearing an elegant dress.

 This cartoon on the front cover of a 1912 edition of *Votes for Women* highlights the fact that women in many parts of the world had already been given the vote.

Newspaper offices

Votes for Women was produced in offices located in the home of the Pethick-Lawrences, who also provided most of the funding. Articles were written by leading members of the WSPU, including Christabel and Sylvia Pankhurst. The newspaper reported all the latest news relating to the struggle for the vote. It started as a monthly newspaper, but demand soon led to it being published weekly, with 30,000 copies a week being sold in 1910.

Army of sellers

To sell the newspaper, the WSPU organised an army of volunteer sellers and an efficient system for delivering the weekly newspaper to newsagents and individual sellers. The paper was sold all across the country. Between 1912 and 1914, sellers often experienced attacks by people reacting to the increasingly extreme actions of militant members of the WSPU.

Women wearing sashes and placards sell *Votes for Women*.

Other newspapers

There were many other suffrage newspapers. *The Women's Suffrage Journal*, edited by Lydia Becker from 1870–1890, was the voice of the suffragists in the 19th century but never gained as many readers as *Votes for Women*. *Common Cause*, published between 1909 and 1920, became the main voice of the NUWSS. The *Vote* was the Women's Freedom League's newspaper, informing supporters and interested people about their campaigns. And organisations which opposed women's suffrage, such as the Women's National Anti-Suffrage League (see page 28), had their own publications, packed with articles attacking the suffrage movement.

The *Suffragette*

In 1912, the Pethick-Lawrences left the WSPU after they fell out with the Pankhursts over the increasingly violent and destructive acts being carried out by members of the WSPU, such as burning buildings to the ground and smashing windows (see pages 38–39). As the Pethick-Lawrences continued to produce *Votes for Women*, the WSPU needed a new newspaper to report on their members' actions. It was edited by Christabel Pankhurst and had the title the *Suffragette*. During the First World War, it changed its title again, to *Britannia*, in support of the government (see pages 40–43).

FUND RAISING AND PROPAGANDA

VOTES FOR WOMEN.

The campaigning organisations needed funds to pay for the rent of offices and for the production of propaganda, such as posters, postcards, pamphlets and other printed material. They also had to pay some workers a wage and, in the case of the WSPU, they needed money to pay women's court fines or lawyers' fees. This rosette in the WSPU colours (see page 27) was pinned to women's clothing. Buying it raised funds for the WSPU, while wearing it brought attention to the cause.

WSPU colours

In 1908 Emmeline Pethick-Lawrence of the WSPU introduced the suffragette colours of purple, white and green. She said, "Purple … stands for the royal blood that flows in the veins of every suffragette … white stands for purity in private and public life … green is the colour of hope and the emblem of spring." The colours also translated into the slogan: Give – green, Women – white, the Vote – violet/purple. The colour scheme was used on items ranging from banners, badges and sashes to posters and tea sets.

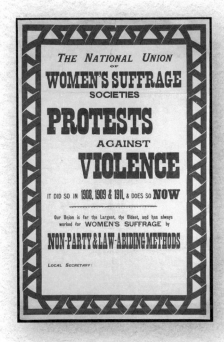

NUWSS colours

The NUWSS also adopted official colours in 1907. At first they were red and white then in 1909 they added green, to translate as the slogan: Give – green, Women – white, Rights – red. They also used their colours on badges, leaflets, posters, pamphlets and banners they produced to increase awareness of the organisation and sold to raise money.

Other suffrage organisations adopted their own colours. The WFL chose a green, white and gold colour scheme (see page 19) while the Artists' Suffrage League used blue and silver. Smart shops realised they could make money by stocking scarves and other fashion items in the colour schemes of the main organisations. Across the country WSPU and NUWSS shops sprang up, run by the local societies.

The border of this poster produced in about 1912 displays the NUWSS colours. The poster indicates the organisation's disapproval of the militant actions of the WSPU.

Postcards

In the early 20th century, there was a craze for sending picture postcards. People sent postcards to make arrangements with friends and family in much the same way as we send text messages. Suffrage organisations used picture postcards as useful propaganda tools. Selling them raised money for the organisations and their presence in the postal system and in people's houses carried their message far and wide.

Many talented artists joined the Suffrage Atelier, founded in 1909, to encourage artists to promote the women's movement 'by means of pictorial publications'. This postcard, also sold as a poster, depicts several respectable women who were denied the vote and some less respectable men who could still be eligible for the vote.

A picture postcard produced by the Suffrage Atelier in 1912 which, like much of their work, highlighted how ridiculous it was that women should be denied the vote.

Organised opposition

Anti-suffrage organisations also used badges, postcards, posters and pamphlets to spread their message. There were several organised groups of women, including the Women's National Anti-Suffrage League, established in 1908, which merged with the Men's League for Opposing Suffrage in 1910 to form the National League for Opposing Woman Suffrage.

Their arguments against votes for women ranged from women not being clever enough to take part in politics, or being too ruled by their emotions, to arguments supporting the idea that society would break down. They argued that if women had the vote they would neglect their children and their household duties or even opt not to have children at all.

> This design appeared on postcards and posters produced by the National League for Opposing Woman Suffrage in 1912.

The Women's Exhibition, 1909

In May 1909, WSPU members organised the Women's Exhibition in the Prince's Skating Rink in Knightsbridge, London. As well as raising money, the WSPU gained a huge amount of publicity by staging such a big event. The exhibition was set out like a village fete or bazaar, with 50 or more stalls selling handmade items and luxury foods. Visitors could also witness a woman acting out a life in the day of an imprisoned suffragette.

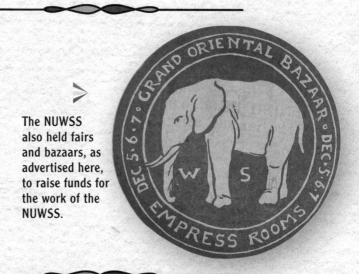

The NUWSS also held fairs and bazaars, as advertised here, to raise funds for the work of the NUWSS.

WSPU fund-raising tour

In 1910 Emmeline Pankhurst set off on a fundraising lecture tour of the USA, where women were campaigning for the vote to be extended to all women across the nation. Several other tours followed, raising thousands of pounds for the WSPU's 'War Chest'. The War Chest was also filled through events such as 'self-denial weeks', when women donated their jewellery or money they would otherwise have spent on luxuries.

> Emmeline Pankhurst sets off from Waterloo Station, London, on her 1911 lecture tour of the USA.

Defaced pennies

Alongside other actions, suffragettes used the brilliant idea of defacing penny coins. This cheap and long-lasting form of propaganda ensured that coins stamped with VOTES FOR WOMEN were passing through people's hands as they went about their daily lives, being seen by a large number of people until the coins were withdrawn from circulation.

It was a criminal act to tamper with coins in circulation, as has occurred here with the words VOTES FOR WOMEN over-stamped across King Edward VII's face.

 The stencil illustrations of the *Anti-suffrage Alphabet* use the WSPU colours of green, white and purple.

Christmas gifts

The suffrage movement produced several board games, books and toys to raise funds and raise awareness of the cause. In 1911, supporters were encouraged to buy copies of the *Anti-suffrage Alphabet* by Laurence Housman as a Christmas gift for female friends and relatives. The verses were illustrated by three of the Suffrage Atelier's female artists, including Ada Ridley, my great-great aunt.

'The March of the Women'

Equally popular with suffragettes and suffragists, the song 'The March of the Women' became the anthem of women campaigners and was dedicated to the WSPU. Composed by Ethel Smyth with words by Cicely Hamilton, women sang the song at meetings, demonstrations and on marches. Its opening words are:

Shout, shout, up with your song!
Cry with the wind for the dawn is breaking.
March, march, swing you along.
Wide blows our banner and hope is waking.

PROCESSIONS, MARCHES AND RALLIES

Across the country, well-dressed women demonstrated their support for women's suffrage by joining marches, processions and rallies. In London the NUWSS and the WSPU staged mass demonstrations involving thousands of participants, starting with the NUWSS's 'Mud March' in February 1907. In 1911, suffrage societies joined together to organise the Coronation Procession. Women who had been to prison for the cause marched in the 'From Prison to Citizenship' section of the procession, see photo right, dressed in fine clothes decorated with WSPU colours.

Showing Asquith

In 1908 the newly elected prime minister, H H Asquith, let it be known that women needed to show him that there was a national demand for women's suffrage. That's why the NUWSS and the WSPU organised big processions in June 1908. Much work went into the planning of the NUWSS procession held on 13 June, including the creation of over 70 hand-stitched fabric banners (see pages 32–33). About 10,000 women marched through London and ended up at a rally held in the Albert Hall.

At the WSPU's Women's Sunday procession a week later, women from across the country gathered at seven meeting places. Then seven processions set off to march through London and join together in Hyde Park. About 300,000 women attended, carrying 700 banners. At the park, women gave speeches from 20 different platforms. Despite these huge peaceful demonstrations of support for women's suffrage, Prime Minister Asquith continued to ignore their demands.

In the 1908 march organised by the NUWSS, suffragists from different cities and towns marched behind banners carrying the name of their town or city, their profession, or a famous woman.

SUFFRAGETTE PROCESSION JUNE 17, 1911.

The Coronation Procession, 1911

During much of 1911 there was a semi-truce between the government and the suffragettes, leaving MPs time to consider the Conciliation Bill (see page 35). However, the impending coronation of King George V gave suffrage societies the reason to join together in the Coronation Procession on 17 June 1911, hoping to gain the new king's support. About 40,000 women marched through London, converging on the Albert Hall for a huge rally. The procession included groups of Scottish, Irish, Welsh and Indian women in national dress.

 Indian women took part in the 1911 procession. Princess Sophia Duleep Singh was among them – she was a leading suffragette.

Women's Suffrage Pilgrimage, 1913

In 1913, the NUWSS organised a mass march to London from cities across the country to remind the general public and the government how much support there was for votes for women and also remind everyone that members of the NUWSS always campaigned peacefully and lawfully. Marchers set off on their pilgrimage from locations all across Britain in June, holding meetings along the way. On 26 July the marchers reached London, marching through the streets to Hyde Park for a rally attended by about 70,000.

BANNERS

F abric banners became a feature of demonstrations, marches and rallies. This banner was designed by the artist, Mary Lowndes, of the Artists' Suffrage League for the NUWSS march in 1908. Alongside banners for towns and cities across Britain, she created designs for different professions (writers, musicians, artists) and ones to celebrate the achievements of great women, such as Florence Nightingale. Nurses in uniform carried this banner and had to hold on tight as it was windy that day, causing the banner to be blown about. It references her nursing work during the Crimean War (1853–56).

Artists' Suffrage League

Mary Lowndes set up the Artists' Suffrage League in order to design and make banners for the first London procession held by the NUWSS in February 1907. The league went on to make many of the banners used by the NUWSS. Part of the idea of banners was to show that women could be feminine, creating beautiful needlework, and yet still be asking for the vote.

Women contributed to banner making in whichever way they could – designing them, sewing them, paying for them or carrying them. Although the Artists' Suffrage League was a centre of banner making, members of local branches of the WSPU or the NUWSS often made their own banners. For instance, Ada Ridley (see page 29) of the Ipswich branch of the WSPU designed and sewed a banner for the 1911 Coronation Procession.

< The banner of the Wimbledon WSPU uses the suffragette colours as well as a local landmark in Wimbledon – a windmill.

Women make pennants and banners at the Artists' Suffrage League headquarters. >

Beyond processions

Although banners were often initially created for a major event, such as a procession, they were reused in many ways. The 76 banners created for the 1908 NUWSS procession went 'on tour' around the country where local suffrage societies set up exhibitions. People paid an entrance fee to view the banners, thus raising money for the cause. Banners were used over and over again, in small local marches and meetings, as well as large events.

Banners used in marches and processions also decorated meeting halls, as here at the WSPU meeting held prior to the 'rush on Parliament' in October 1908. >

NO VOTE, NO CENSUS

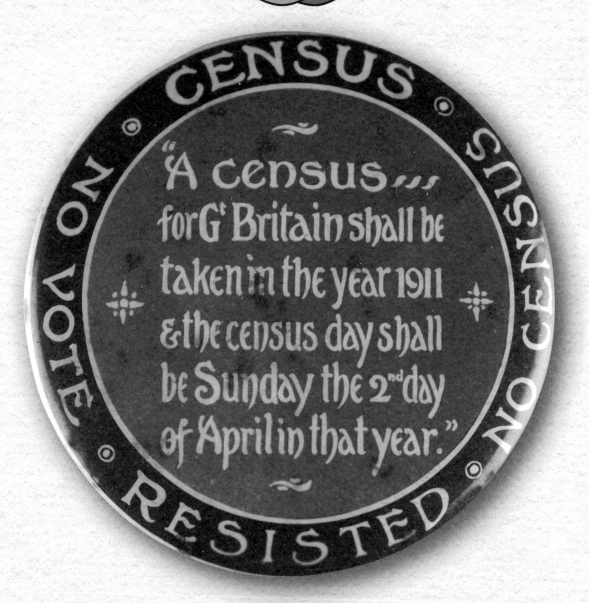

"A census... for Gt Britain shall be taken in the year 1911 & the census day shall be Sunday the 2nd day of April in that year."

CENSUS · NO VOTE · NO CENSUS · RESISTED · NO CENSUS · ON

The British government had been collecting information about all the people in the United Kingdom every ten years since 1801 by organising a census. In 1911, another census was due. Members of the Women's Tax Resistance League, the WFL and the WSPU joined together to plan a protest linked to the 1911 census. They stated: if women don't count, neither shall they be counted. This metal badge was worn to encourage others to join the protest.

The Conciliation Bill

A second Conciliation Bill was due for consideration by the Houses of Parliament during 1911. Part of the reason for the census protest was to keep up the pressure on the Liberal government to pass the Conciliation Bill in the hope that, even if it only gave the vote to a small group of women, soon the rest would be given the same rights.

1911 Census

The Liberal government included extra questions on the 1911 census schedule (form) as government ministers were keen to collect information about the population's welfare and health to support their proposed health reforms. This meant that alongside the usual information, recording exactly who was present in the household on the evening of census night, 2 April 1911, the head of the household was asked to provide details of how many children had been born in the marriage, and whether any had died in childbirth or childhood.

Ways to protest

The census protest was to take two forms. The first involved resisting the census. Women householders were encouraged to spoil the census form by writing something like VOTES FOR WOMEN across the document (below), or to persuade their husbands not to record them. It was against the law to refuse to fill in the census form so this action could have led to a £5 fine, or a prison sentence if the fine wasn't paid. The other form of protest was not illegal as such, but involved evading the census by being away from home on the night of the census.

Census night

On the night of 2 April some women spoiled the census and many others evaded it by being away from home. Some attended census evaders' parties up and down the country while others hid in their friends' houses. Emily Wilding Davison, see next page, was discovered in a cupboard in the Houses of Parliament, while other women went on walks in the countryside, disappearing into the night.

After census night had passed, the government claimed that the protest had not been successful and the organisers claimed the opposite. What can be said is that it brought a great deal of attention to the issue of votes for women.

▽ A few evaders made the front page of the *Daily Sketch* when they slept in caravans on Wimbledon Common, London on 2 April, 1911.

Suffragettes and suffragists were divided on whether to support the protest. In January 1911 the NUWSS officially decided not to support census evasion, even though it did not break the law. For working women or women in positions of responsibility, they had to weigh up whether their job was at risk and whether they could afford to pay the £5 fine if they spoiled the form.

DERBY DAY, 1913

DAILY SKETCH.

No. 1,323—THURSDAY, JUNE 5, 1913.　Longacre 40-47, Fleet-lane, E.C.　MANCHESTER: Withy-grove.　　　(Registered as a Newspaper.)　**ONE HALFPENNY.**

HISTORY'S MOST WONDERFUL DERBY: FIRST HORSE DISQUALIFIED: A 100 TO 1 CHANCE WINS: SUFFRAGETTE NEARLY KILLED BY THE KING'S COLT.

Miss Emily Davison.　　The woman falling to the ground.　　The King's horse, Anmer, falls on his jockey.　　Herbert Jones.

Yesterday's Derby was extraordinary. Not only was Craganour, the favourite, disqualified after finishing first, the race being awarded to Aboyeur; a suffragette ran across the course at Tattenham Corner and seized the bridle of the King's horse. The King's horse and jockey were thrown to the ground, while the woman was nearly killed. The extraordinary photograph seen above was taken by the Daily Sketch a second after the horse and the woman fell to the ground.

On Derby Day 1913, Emily Wilding Davison became one of the most famous suffragettes in history when she slipped under the rails of Epsom racecourse and stepped in front of Anmer, the racehorse owned by King George V. The horse trampled Emily, threw its jockey and turned a somersault. This awful event was recorded on newsreel and reported in newspapers in Great Britain and across the world, including the *Daily Sketch*. Four days later Emily Wilding Davison died of her injuries.

Emily Wilding Davison

Born in 1872, Emily studied at university before becoming a governess and teacher. She joined the WSPU in 1906 and gave up her job as a teacher three years later to devote herself to campaigning for votes for women. Following the WSPU motto of 'Deeds not Words', she carried out many actions to draw attention to the cause, often acting alone. She set light to post boxes and buildings, smashed windows, assaulted a man she mistook for the MP, David Lloyd George, and caused public disturbances. As a result, she went to prison nine times and she was force fed on a number of occasions. She was one of the suffragettes who was prepared to take part in increasingly destructive, militant acts as time passed and women still did not gain the vote.

Derby Day, 1913

Huge crowds were gathered at Epsom racecourse on Derby Day, 4 June 1913. When Emily stepped in front of King George V's horse, Anmer, she knew that thousands of people would see her actions. Some historians think she intended to sacrifice her life while others think she was trying to attach a WSPU flag to the bridle of Anmer. Evidence to support this view comes from the fact that a few days before Derby Day, a small group of women, including Emily, were seen practising how to catch hold of the bridles of horses trotting in circles. In addition, her return train ticket was found in her purse and she had plans for attending events in the future. Whichever version of events is true, she was prepared to take the risk that she would be injured and might not survive.

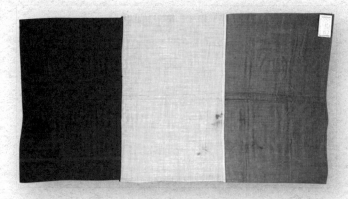

⚠ This WSPU flag and another identical one were found inside Emily Wilding Davison's coat when she reached hospital. (Below) Emily's train ticket.

Funeral

After Emily's death, the WSPU were quick to turn her into a martyr. They organised a huge funeral procession to accompany her coffin on its way through London. In front of the coffin, women carried a purple banner with the words: FIGHT ON & GOD WILL GIVE THE VICTORY. After a memorial service, the coffin travelled by train to Northumberland for a private family funeral the following day. The WSPU motto 'Deeds not Words' is engraved on Emily's gravestone.

SCALING UP THE ACTION

Emily Wilding Davison's protest action in 1913 was one of hundreds carried out by suffragettes between 1912 and 1914. Furious at the failure of the Conciliation Bill in 1912, Emmeline Pankhurst encouraged suffragettes to do as much damage as they could, in a bid to force the government to give women the vote. The private homes of several politicians became a focus for attacks, including the seaside home of MP Arthur du Cros in St Leonards, Hastings, seen here still smouldering after women set light to it in April 1913.

Arson

Suffragettes across the country set light to letters in post boxes and burnt down churches, sports pavilions, railway stations and race courses. They burnt messages such as NO VOTE NO GOLF onto golf greens, and bombed a house being built for MP David Lloyd George. Suffragettes always made sure that buildings were empty of people and pets.

Mass smash

In March 1912 a mass window-smashing campaign took place. In a planned action, about 150 women made their way to some of London's smartest shopping streets and government buildings and shattered the windows by throwing stones or hitting the glass with toffee hammers. Most of the women were immediately arrested.

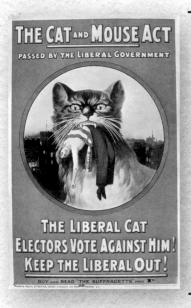

Cat and Mouse

While some suffragettes evaded capture, the prisons were filling up with hunger-striking suffragettes. To deal with this problem, the government swiftly passed the Prisoners' Temporary Discharge for Ill-Health Act in April 1913. Quickly labelled the 'Cat and Mouse Act', it removed the need for force feeding by allowing prison governors to temporarily release hunger strikers, only for them to be re-arrested when they had regained some health. This prevented death but didn't stop women from becoming extremely weak and ill.

A WSPU poster of the time shows a fierce cat (representing the police, prisons and the government) holding an injured suffragette 'mouse' in its mouth.

Under surveillance

After suffragettes took their protest into museums and galleries, the government put certain individuals under police surveillance. They also banned the WSPU from holding open-air meetings, raided WSPU offices and confiscated their funds. Members of the WSPU were increasingly forced to go under cover, especially the Pankhursts.

This surveillance photograph was issued to museums and galleries to help them identify militant suffragettes. Mary Richardson, number 11, slashed the _Rokeby Venus_ in the National Gallery in 1914.

Help or hindrance?

Unfortunately for the cause, politicians, including those who had once supported women's suffrage, reacted angrily to WSPU arson and other criminal acts, as did members of the NUWSS. Their membership had grown enormously to over 100,000 by 1914 and they felt their work was being undermined by the WSPU. Sylvia Pankhurst and the East London Federation of Suffragettes, a mostly working class organisation, also decided to reject the WSPU's violent methods to focus on social reform, working closely with the Labour Party.

THE FIRST WORLD WAR

On 4 August 1914, Britain declared war on Germany and Austria-Hungary, joining the war on the side of France, Belgium and Russia. Soon thousands of British men marched off to war, leaving families, everyday life and jobs behind them. Crowds of men, women and children gathered to wave off soldiers, as here in the market place of Lavenham, Suffolk on 5 August 1914.

The WSPU reacts to war

Up until war broke out, members of the WSPU had been causing as much trouble as they could for the government. When war broke out, Christabel Pankhurst declared that the war was God's vengeance upon those men who had refused equality to women. However, very quickly a deal was struck leading to the release of all suffragette prisoners on the understanding that WSPU violence would stop. Immediately the Pankhursts and the WSPU threw themselves into support for the war effort and stopped campaigning for votes for women.

The NUWSS reacts

Millicent Garrett Fawcett and the NUWSS, like most female campaigners for the vote, had campaigned for peace prior to the outbreak of war. Members of the NUWSS took part in the peace rally that took place just hours before war was declared. However, Millicent was warned that she shouldn't link the NUWSS with pacifists or the organisation would lose support among MPs, so they too agreed to suspend the suffrage campaign.

Peace movement

While the leaders of the NUWSS and the WSPU may have decided to officially support the war effort, large numbers of their members did not agree. Some became involved in the international women's movement across Europe whose aim was to bring the opposing countries together to talk through their differences and bring Europe to peace.

In 1915 there was an International Congress of Women in The Hague, the Netherlands, attended by 1,200 women from 12 countries, who met to discuss ways to bring about peace.

Women's Service Bureau

Almost immediately the NUWSS set up its Women's Service Bureau to match female volunteers to all sorts of voluntary war work. Women went to work for charities that were supporting the troops, helping refugees or providing volunteer nurses. The bureau also set up training courses for women to become welders, for instance, so that women could take on jobs in aircraft and munitions factories.

During the war thousands of women worked in munitions factories. It was dangerous as they were working with poisonous, explosive chemicals.

Women's Right to Serve

In 1915, the government found themselves working with Emmeline Pankhurst and the WSPU, rather than against them, providing funds for them to organise the Women's Right to Serve March through London in July 1915. The point of the march was to show women's willingness to support the war effort through work, and also help recruit more men into the armed forces and more women into war work. In particular there was a desperate need for women to work in munitions factories to help deal with a terrible shortage of ammunition in 1915.

Hospitals and nursing

At first women who offered their services as nurses or doctors to care for wounded soldiers were told to go home. Undeterred, some set off anyway, including Dr Elsie Inglis. She set up hospital units abroad, close to battlefronts, which were funded by suffrage societies and staffed by women. During the course of the war, thousands of women worked as military nurses, volunteer nurses or even ambulance drivers.

V Nurses who worked in the Voluntary Aid Detachments linked to the Red Cross provided basic care to ill, wounded and dying soldiers.

In 1917 the government set up the Women's Land Army to provide an extra workforce to farmers.

The war effort

Whether or not women supported Britain's decision to go to war, they quickly found themselves contributing to the war effort in one way or another. Filling the gaps in the workforce left by men who had joined the armed forces, women worked on the buses and on the railways, as mechanics and factory workers, they delivered the post and did farm work. At home women had to step into the place of their husbands or fathers, running the household. As the war wore on, they made food stretch further as the country struggled to feed everyone once ships bringing food from abroad began to be attacked by German submarines.

NATIONAL SERVICE WOMEN'S LAND ARMY

GOD SPEED THE PLOUGH AND THE WOMAN WHO DRIVES IT

APPLY FOR ENROLMENT FORMS AT YOUR NEAREST POST OFFICE OR EMPLOYMENT EXCHANGE

Women's Army Auxiliary Corps

The Women's Army Auxiliary Corps (WAAC) was set up in 1916 to release more men to fight abroad, while women stepped into their roles in the army. Along with all the jobs listed on this poster, women worked at the cemeteries springing up across France. The navy and the air force set up similar organisations – the Women's Royal Naval Service and the Women's Royal Air Force.

Campaign for votes continues

It had come as a huge shock to many suffragettes and suffragists when both the main organisations decided to halt the campaign and support the war effort. Resignations followed and some women continued to work for peace and campaign for votes, including Sylvia Pankhurst and her East London Federation of Suffragettes, renamed the Workers' Suffrage Federation in 1916. The Women's Freedom League also continued to campaign throughout the war. When the issue of voting rights was again being debated in Parliament in 1916, Millicent Garrett Fawcett and the NUWSS quickly became involved, helping to press the case for the vote to be extended to women this time.

Government's dilemma

Politicians realised that thousands of men serving in the armed forces would be disqualified from voting in the next general election as they had not been resident at their home address for a year or more. In a bid to right this wrong, MPs started to debate the Representation of the People Bill, which also brought the issue of votes for women to the fore once more. Finally, the majority of politicians seemed to be in favour of women's suffrage, at least partly due to women's war work.

A recruitment poster lists many of the roles that women undertook in the WAAC.

Liberal politician David Lloyd George, who became prime minister in 1916, had always been more in favour of women's suffrage than his predecessor, H H Asquith.

THE VOTE!

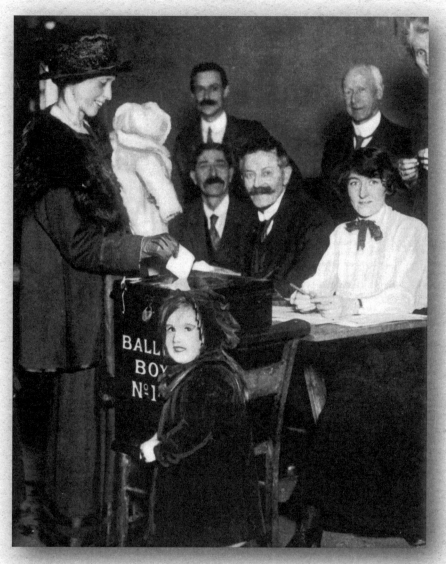

In February 1918, before the war had ended, the Representation of the People Act became law. Finally women over the age of 30 who owned a house, or were married to someone who did, had the right to vote. The act also gave the vote to all men of 21 or over, and to men of 19 and over who were serving in the armed forces. After the Armistice on 11 November 1918 brought the fighting to a halt, there was a general election in December. Women voted for the first time, as this mother is doing while the election officers pose for the camera.

Young women miss out

About 21.4 million people were now eligible to vote, of which about 8.5 million were women, representing about 40 per cent of adult women. However, the very women who had worked so hard to keep the country going during the war were mostly under 30 and so did not get the vote. Still, their efforts had helped to persuade MPs that women deserved the vote by showing that women were reliable, efficient, hard-working, brave, strong and equal to men in many jobs.

Women as MPs

The year 1918 also saw Parliament pass an act allowing women to stand as candidates for election to Parliament. Christabel Pankhurst and 16 other women stood as candidates but only one was elected. She was called Countess Markievicz and she did not take up her seat as she stood for Sinn Fein, a political movement who wanted a united, independent Ireland. The first woman to become an MP and take up her seat was Viscountess Nancy Astor, who was elected to Parliament in 1919.

Nancy Astor campaigning for votes prior to the Plymouth by-election in 1919. Her husband was MP for Plymouth before she won the seat.

National Union for Equal Citizenship

In 1919 Millicent Garrett Fawcett retired as president of the NUWSS and at the same meeting the NUWSS became the National Union for Equal Citizenship. The organisation continued to campaign to lower the voting age for women, but also took on other struggles, such as women being treated fairly by the law and in the workplace. The struggle for equal opportunities and equal pay for women continues to this day.

After the war

More than a million women had joined the workforce between 1914 and 1918. After the war ended, men returned to their homes and their jobs. Many women lost the skilled jobs they had been doing and returned to the home, or to less skilled 'women's work', such as cleaning and cooking. There were more opportunities for some, as lawyers or other professional jobs, but for others life was tough, especially if husbands or sons had died or been injured during the war.

Equal rights, 1928

It was not until 1928 that the Equal Franchise Act gave the vote to women of 21 and over. Thousands of people, male and female, had helped women win the vote but some historians think that the WSPU's tactics may have slowed things down. Perhaps the law-abiding, peaceful NUWSS campaigners should take more of the credit, alongside women's war work. Millicent Garrett Fawcett (below, front passenger) lived to see the victory and to enjoy the celebrations that followed.

GLOSSARY

Act Short for an act of Parliament, which creates a new law or changes an existing law.

Amendment A change made to an existing law.

Armistice An agreement between opposing sides in a war to stop fighting while a peace treaty is discussed.

Arson To deliberately set fire to someone's house or other private property.

Artists' Suffrage League Set up in 1907, the organisation drew together artists to design and produce large numbers of posters, banners and postcards for the NUWSS.

Bailiff An official who takes away a debtor's money or goods to the same value as what they owe.

Ballot paper A small piece of paper used to mark someone's voting preference.

Banner A long piece of fabric, usually carrying a message or a logo, hung from a pole, or between two poles.

Bill A draft of a law presented to the Houses of Parliament for discussion.

By-election An election held to fill a vacancy when an MP has to resign or dies.

Campaign A set of actions organised to achieve a particular goal, such as votes for women.

Cat and Mouse Act/Prisoner's Temporary Discharge of Ill Health Act The act that allowed prison governors to release hunger strikers from prison and then re-arrest them to complete their sentence once they had regained some strength.

Census An official count of the population of a country on a single date.

Committee A group of people within an organisation.

Conciliation Bill There were several versions of this bill in 1910–1911 proposing that wealthy women who owned property should have the right to vote. Despite discussion in Parliament during which it gained support from the majority of MPs, Prime Minister Asquith blocked its progress towards becoming an act in 1910 and 1911.

Conservative Party (also called the Tory Party) One of the two main political parties in Britain in the 19th and early 20th centuries.

Contagious Diseases Acts During the 1860s, these acts were introduced to try to reduce the spread of sexually transmitted diseases in men. Josephine Butler campaigned for them to be overturned as the acts gave permission for police to stop any woman who was out late at night, and punished women, not men.

Crimean War The war between Russia on one side and Britain, France, Sardinia and Turkey on the other that took place between 1853 and 1856 in the Crimean peninsula, close to the Russian-Turkish border.

Democratic Supporting democracy – equal treatment of people's views and rights.

Deputation A group of people sent to represent the views of others.

Derby Day A famous horse race held at Epsom Racecourse on the first Saturday in June each year.

Downing Street A famous street in London; the official home of the British prime minister is 10 Downing Street.

East London Federation of Suffragettes Originally the East London branch of the WSPU, set up by Sylvia Pankhurst, it changed its name to the East London Federation of Suffragettes when Sylvia was expelled from the WSPU in 1914.

Election The official selection of someone to a political or other position by voting.

Electoral register (or roll) The official list of people who have the right to vote in general elections.

Electorate All the people in an area or a country who have the right to vote in an election.

First World War The war that lasted from 1914 to 1918, fought by Britain, France, Russia, the USA and others on one side against Germany, Austria-Hungary and others on the other.

Force feeding Hunger strikers were often force fed, which meant that a feeding tube was pushed down their throat or up their nose against their wishes, so that food could be poured directly into the stomach.

Founding member One of the people who sets up, or founds, a society or organisation.

Franchise The right to vote in public elections.

General election The official election of representatives ie Members of Parliament, to the House of Commons.

Great Reform Act In 1832, this act extended the vote to a greater proportion of the male population and gave some unrepresented areas of the country an MP to represent them.

Holloway From 1902, this was a women-only prison in London. Many suffragettes were imprisoned there for breaking the law.

House of Commons One of two parts that make up the UK Parliament. Members of Parliament are elected to represent the interests of the people who vote for them in the House of Commons.

House of Lords One of two parts that make up the UK Parliament. Members are unelected and include bishops and peers, and people who have inherited the right to sit in the House of Lords.

Houses of Parliament The House of Commons and the House of Lords, also referred to often simply as Parliament.

Hunger striker A prisoner who refuses to eat as a protest.

Independent Labour Party A socialist political party set up in 1893 that eventually became the Labour Party in 1906.

Ladies Gallery A small space, high above the House of Commons chamber, where women were allowed to watch MPs discussing matters of government in the 19th and early 20th centuries.

Liberal Party One of the two main political parties in the 19th and early 20th centuries.

Local election A local election decides who runs local councils.

Member of Parliament (MP) Someone elected to the House of Commons as a representative of the people living in a particular area of the country.

Militant Violent, forceful or aggressive action or behaviour to further a cause or belief.

Mill worker Someone who worked in a mill (factory) that made cloth.

Motto A short sentence or phrase that sums up the aims or beliefs of an organisation.

National League for Opposing Woman Suffrage The organisation that actively campaigned against women's suffrage.

National Union of Women's Suffrage Societies (NUWSS) The national suffrage society formed in 1897, bringing together many smaller suffrage societies.

Pamphlet A small booklet or leaflet.

Pennant A long fabric flag, often triangular.

Petition A written request signed by many people and presented to an MP. Petitions were, and remain, a way for citizens to suggest topics for debate in Parliament.

Pilgrimage A long journey made for a special reason.

Politician Someone who is heavily involved in politics and government, especially an MP.

Portcullis A strong, heavy, metal grate that can be lowered to block a gateway or doorway.

Prime minister The most important elected government minister, head of the ruling party.

Prison governor The official appointed to run a prison.

Propaganda Information used to promote a particular idea or cause.

Property qualification Here, ownership of property that gives the right to vote.

Rally A mass meeting.

Sash A long strip of cloth worn across the body.

School Board The group of people responsible for running local schools.

Scroll A document formed from a long piece of paper, or several long pieces of paper, fixed together, and then rolled up.

Sphere Here, an area of life, such as domestic life (home and family) or public life (politics and business).

Suffrage The power to vote.

Suffrage Atelier A group of artists who worked closely with the WFL and the WSPU.

Suffragette A campaigner for votes for women, many of whom were prepared to carry out militant acts, and usually referring to members of the WSPU.

Suffragist A campaigner for votes for women who used lawful and peaceful methods. Men and women were suffragists.

Toffee hammer A small hammer that formed part of the equipment of an Edwardian kitchen. It was used to break up blocks of homemade toffee.

Universal suffrage Equal voting rights for men and women.

Vanning Short for caravanning. Several suffrage organisations sent women out on caravan, or vanning, tours of the countryside to spread the word about votes for women.

Volunteer Someone who willingly works and receives no payment for their work.

Westminster Hall The oldest building in the Houses of Parliament.

Women's Freedom League The militant but not violent women's suffrage organisation formed in 1907.

Women's Social and Political Union (WSPU) The militant women's suffrage campaigning organisation set up in 1903 by Emmeline Pankhurst.

Women's Tax Resistance League The tax resistance organisation linked to the Women's Freedom League and set up in 1909.

TIMELINE AND INDEX

1792 Mary Wollstonecraft's book *A Vindication of the Rights of Woman* argued that women should be given access to education and better rights.

1832 The Great Reform Act extended the vote to a wider group of mostly middle-class men, but <u>not</u> women.

1866 Women organised the Petition asking for votes for women.

1867 J S Mill tried to persuade MPs to amend (change) the 1867 Reform Bill but was unsuccessful. The first women's suffrage societies were set up.

1869 In local elections, a few female property owners were given the right to vote.

1870 The Women's Suffrage Bill, the first of many, was rejected by Parliament. That year, the law changed to allow married women to own property.

1884 Suffrage societies campaigned for women to be given the vote through the Third Reform Act.

1894 The Local Government Act gave all women the right to vote and stand for election at a local level (parish councils, district councils etc).

1897 The National Union of Women's Suffrage Societies (NUWSS) united many suffrage societies.

1903 The Women's Social and Political Union (WSPU) was founded by Emmeline Pankhurst.

1905 The first WSPU militant act.

1906 The Liberal Party won the general election.

1907 The Women's Freedom League (WFL) was set up.

1908 Henry Asquith became prime minister. The NUWSS and the WSPU organised marches.

1909 The Women's Exhibition was held by the WSPU. Force feeding of hunger strikers began.

1910–1912 Several Conciliation Bills, which would have given the vote to some women, were considered. 10 November: Black Friday.

1911 The census protest. Women's Coronation Procession.

1912 Members of the WSPU carried out increasingly violent or destructive acts.

1913 Prisoners' Temporary Discharge for Ill-Health Act or 'Cat and Mouse' Act. Emily Wilding Davison died.

1914 Suffragette militant action was at its height. 4 August: Britain joined the war; millions of women joined the war effort. The votes for women campaign mostly stopped.

1918 February: Representation of the People Act – women over 30 were able to vote in general elections. November: women were allowed to stand for election as MPs.

1919 Lady Astor became the first female MP. The Sex Disqualification (Removal) Act made it illegal for women to be prevented from working in various jobs because they were women or married.

1928 Equal Franchise Act granted equal voting rights.

1969 Voting age lowered to 18 for men and women.

1970 Equal Pay Act.

1975 The Sex Discrimination Act protected men and women from discrimination in all areas of life.

1979 Margaret Thatcher – first female prime minister.

1992 Betty Boothroyd became the first female Speaker of the House of Commons.

Today The percentage of women MPs is still a third of the total number of MPs. Women still campaign for equal opportunities and equal pay.

Anderson, Elizabeth Garrett 6, 8–9, 11, 13, 17
anti-suffragists 12, 25, 28
Artists' Suffrage League 27, 32–33
Asquith, H H 6, 16, 19, 21, 30, 43
Astor, Viscountess Nancy 6, 45

banners 18, 27, 29–33, 37
Becker, Lydia 6, 11, 12, 25
Billington-Greig, Teresa 6, 19
Black Friday 21
Bright, Jacob 12
brooches/badges 14, 19, 21, 27, 28, 34

'Cat and Mouse Act' 39
census, 1911 19, 34–35
chain and padlock protests 18–21
coins, defaced 29
colours, official 19, 24, 26–27, 29, 30, 33
Conciliation Bill 21, 31, 35, 38
Conservative Party 12

Davies, Emily 6, 8–9, 11
Davison, Emily Wilding 6, 35–38
Despard, Charlotte 6, 16, 19
Drummond, Flora 6, 16–17, 20
Duval, Elsie 22–23

East London Federation of Suffragettes 7, 39, 43
education (for girls/women) 5, 6, 11, 13
Equal Franchise Act 45

Fawcett, Millicent Garrett 6, 9–11, 13, 17, 41, 43, 45
First World War 7, 25, 40–45
force feeding 7, 22–23, 37, 39
fund raising 16, 19, 26–29, 33

Gladstone, William 12
Great Reform Act 5

Housman, Laurence 7, 29

Independent Labour Party (ILP) 6, 12, 15

Kenney, Annie 7, 15, 16
King George V 6, 31, 36–37

Liberal Party 6, 7, 12, 15, 23, 35, 43
Lloyd George, David 7, 37, 39, 43
Lowndes, Mary 32–33
Lytton, Lady Constance 7, 23

Manchester National Society 6, 11–12
marches 19, 29, 30–33, 42

Markievicz, Countess 45
Matters, Muriel 19
medals, hunger-strike 22–23
Mill, J S 7–9, 12

National League for Opposing Woman Suffrage 28
National Union for Equal Citizenship 45
National Union of Women's Suffrage Societies (NUWSS) 6, 10, 13, 15, 17, 19, 25, 27–28, 30–33, 35, 39, 41, 43, 45
New, Edith 17, 20–21
newspapers, suffrage 6, 7, 16–17, 19, 24–25

Pankhursts
Christabel 7, 14–17, 19, 25, 39, 41, 45
Emmeline 6, 7, 14–17, 19, 28, 38–39, 41–42
Sylvia 7, 14–16, 21, 25, 39, 41, 43
Peterloo Massacre 5
Pethick-Lawrences 7, 16, 19, 24–25, 27
Petition (1866) 6–11, 17
postcards 4, 9, 19, 26–28
prison 7, 15, 17, 20–23, 28, 30, 35, 37, 39, 41
processions 6–7, 16, 19, 30–33
propaganda 11, 15, 16, 19, 24–29

Queen Victoria 7, 12

rallies 30–33
Representation of the People Act 7, 43–45

Second Reform Act 9
Singh, Princess Sophia Duleep 7, 31
sphere, private/public 5
strikes, hunger 22–23, 37, 39
Suffrage Atelier 7, 27, 29

Third Reform Act 12

Votes for Women 7, 16, 24–25

Women's Army Auxiliary Corps 43
Women's Freedom League (WFL) 6, 9, 17–20, 25, 27, 34–35, 43
Women's Land Army 42
Women's Social and Political Union (WSPU) 6–7, 14–17, 19–39, 41–43, 45
Women's Tax Resistance League 19, 34–35